J. Im

J. Imrich

Better Homes and Gardens®

DAY AND NIGHT

Hi! My name is Max.
I have some great projects
to show you—some about day and
some about night! We're going
to have lots of fun making
them together.

Inside You'll Find...

Look for unusual things in Max's kitchen.

Wake Up, Max!

Max noticed that the "P" on his pepper shaker is backward. Can you point out the 10 other things that are wrong in Max's kitchen?

Freshly baked biscuits are made to look like little golden suns.

Sunshine Breakfast Biscuits

Rise and shine! When you get up in the morning, do you like to eat breakfast? Max is always ready to eat, especially after he helps make and bake these easy biscuits.

What you'll need...

- 1 package (10) refrigerator biscuits
- Shortening
- Cookie sheet

- Table knife
- Orange marmalade or your favorite jam or jelly

- Measuring spoons
- Hot pads
- Pancake turner

1 With adult help, preheat the oven to 450°. Break open the tube of biscuits, separate the biscuits, and place them on a greased cookie sheet. Pat each biscuit into a 3-inch circle.

To make the sun design, use the knife to press the sun's "rays" into each biscuit.

2 Press your thumb into the center of each biscuit to make a thumbprint hole.

3 Drop about ½ teaspoon of orange marmalade into the center of each biscuit. Bake for 6 to 8 minutes or until golden.

With adult help, use hot pads to remove the cookie sheet from the oven. With a pancake turner, lift biscuits off the cookie sheet and onto a plate. Serve warm.

Bravo for Breakfast!

These fresh-from-the-oven jelly biscuits taste great. But don't stop there. Eat them with your favorite fruit—grapes, berries, apple slices, or melon. Then wash everything down with a big glass of cold milk. What a great way to begin any day!

Use small pieces of yellow plastic foam to design a sun mosaic.

Smiling Sun

This sun looks very happy about something. Why do you think it has such a big smile? What makes you smile?

What you'll need...

- Scissors
- Yellow construction paper
- White crafts glue
- Blue construction paper
- Crayon or marker
- Yellow plastic foam containers (egg cartons)

1 For the sun's head, cut a big circle from the yellow construction paper. Glue the circle on the blue construction paper.

Use a crayon to draw a happy sun face. Draw sun rays all around the circle (see photo).

2 Tear the foam containers into small pieces.

3 Dot glue onto one of the sun's rays. Firmly press the foam pieces onto the glue. Keep gluing and pressing the pieces on the paper until you finish all the rays. Let the sun dry overnight.

Match the animals with their shadows.

Shadows

Max likes to watch the shadows that show up in the bright sunlight, but he wishes the sun weren't quite so hot. Next time you're outside on a sunshiny day, look for your shadow.

Shadow Search

Did you know that your shadow looks different from your friend's shadow? In fact, shadows from different people or animals look quite different.

Look below at the pictures of a buffalo, deer, dog, horse, and eagle. Then point to the shadow picture that goes with each one.

Fingers and a good imagination make great shadow creatures.

Shadow Pictures

Have you ever tried to make a bird shadow? It's fun and so easy to do. Max moves his hands back and forth so the shadow bird flaps its wings. Can you do that?

What you'll need...
- Bright source of light or flashlight
- Wall or large piece of cardboard

Animal Shadows

Look at the shadows on page 13. Can you hold your hand as shown in the photos to make all of the Shadow Pictures?

Can you wiggle your fingers for a rabbit's or horse's ears? Can you fly like a bird, bark like a dog, or quack like a duck?

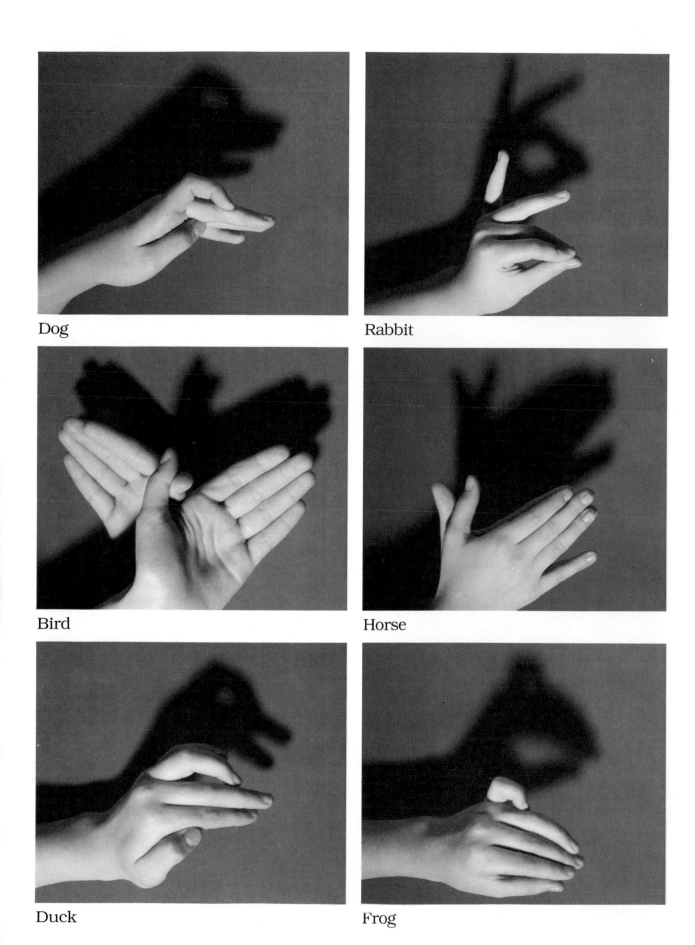

Dog

Rabbit

Bird

Horse

Duck

Frog

Simple-to-do puppets make for an entertaining shadow show.

Shadow Puppets

Paper puppets are lots of fun because you can draw them any shape you like. And, their shadows can be any size you like. Can you make shadows on the wall that are big and small?

What you'll need...

- Construction paper or lightweight cardboard
- Crayon or pencil
- Tape
- Scissors
- Crafts sticks or drinking straws
- Lamp or flashlight

1 With a crayon, draw simple shapes any way you like on a piece of paper. Do you want to make shapes from nursery rhymes or your favorite story?

2 Use the scissors to cut out your shapes.

3 Securely tape a crafts stick to the back side of each shape.

Now turn on the lamp, shine the light on a wall, and you're ready to give your own shadow puppet show.

Puppet Play

It's time for a shadow show! Hold your puppets by their sticks. Place the puppets near a bright light. Make sure your puppets are between the light and a wall. Now look at the wall to see your puppets' shadows. Move the puppets so their shadows move.

Sleep Tight, Max

Max is getting ready to go to sleep. All the lights are turned off, except for one. Why has he left it on? Can you name all the lights in Max's bedroom?

STOP DRAGON COUNTRY

Decorate empty milk or juice cartons to look like your house.

Little-House Night-Light

Have you ever gone outside when it's dark to see what your home looks like? If you build this carton house and then shine a flashlight into it, that's how your home looks at night.

What you'll need...

- Little-House carton (see page 31)
- One 9x12-inch piece construction paper
- Tape
- Crayons or markers
- Crafts knife or small knife
- 1 rectangular piece construction paper
- White crafts glue
- Flashlight

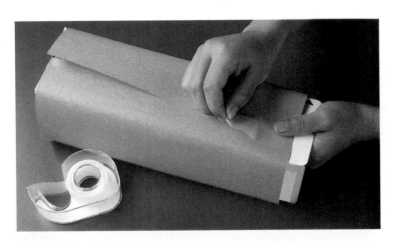

1 Lay the Little-House carton on the piece of construction paper. Wrap the paper around the carton. Tape the paper in place (see photo).

Close the carton's top by tucking the sides back into place. Tape the carton top closed.

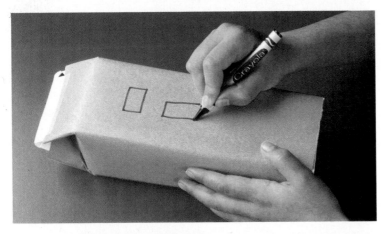

2 Use a crayon to draw 3 or 4 windows and 1 or 2 doors on your house.

With adult help, carefully use the crafts knife to cut out the windows and doors.

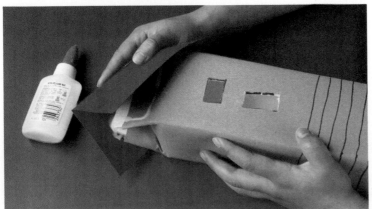

3 For the house's roof, fold the rectangular piece of construction paper in half. Glue the roof to the top of the carton.

Now decorate your house any way you like.

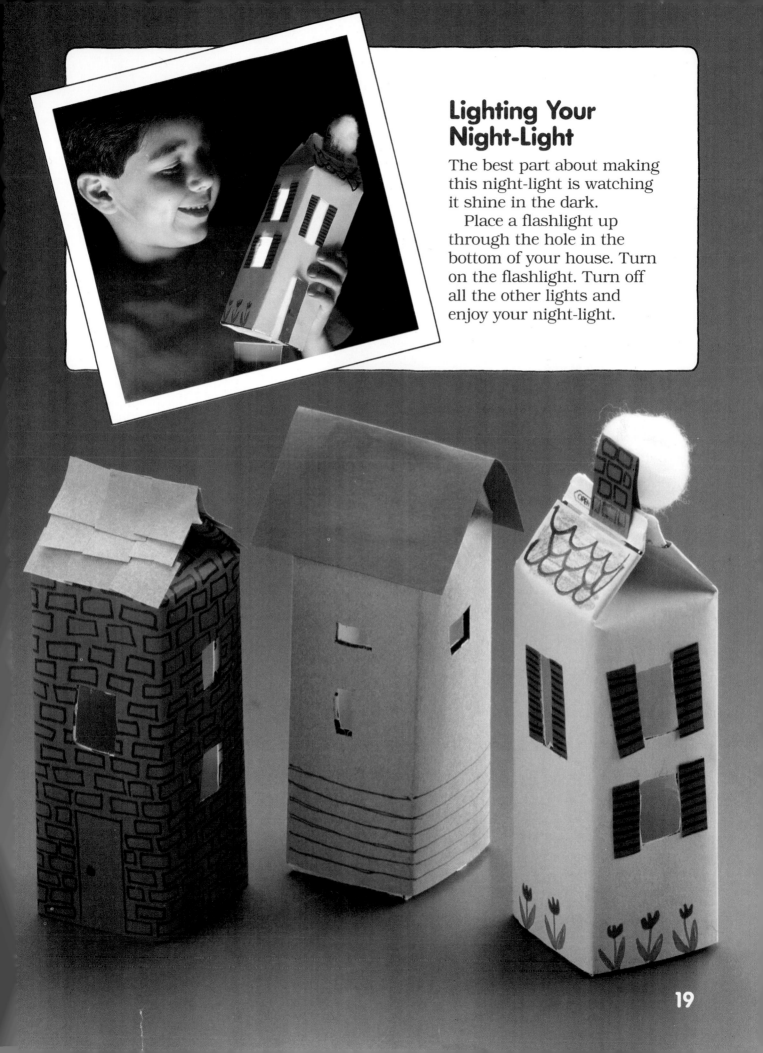

Lighting Your Night-Light

The best part about making this night-light is watching it shine in the dark.

Place a flashlight up through the hole in the bottom of your house. Turn on the flashlight. Turn off all the other lights and enjoy your night-light.

The sky's the limit when it comes to creating things with clay.

Moon Faces

Have you ever heard of the man in the moon? Some people say when you look at the moon, you can almost see his face. But you don't need to wait until nighttime to make these faces!

What you'll need...

- Tape
- Waxed paper
- Salt Dough (see page 31)
- Shortening
- Cookie sheet

1 Tape waxed paper on the counter. Mold a large piece of Salt Dough into a moon shape that is ½ to ¾ inch thick.

2 Roll tiny pieces of Salt Dough into balls and ropes and place on large moon shape to make a face. Press with thumb to make cheeks. Or, make any face you like.

3 Carefully remove the clay faces from the waxed paper and place onto a lightly greased cookie sheet. With adult help, bake as directed on page 31.

If you would like to make a hanging ornament, insert a paper clip into the dough before baking (see the face in the bottom row on the next page).

Hunt for the night creatures that are visiting Max.

Night Creatures

Max is camping out in his tent. After dark, he notices that he has several nighttime visitors. Max is telling the fireflies, moths, bats, owls, and raccoon good-night.

Counting Fun

Max's campsite is home to lots of animals and bugs. They sleep during the day and are awake at nighttime. While Max sleeps, they will be having fun.

The numbers below show how many of each creature are around Max's tent. Can you point to each one?

1 Raccoon

2 Owls

3 Bats

4 Moths

5 Fireflies

This art technique, called crayon engraving, is always a big hit.

Firefly Scratch-Off Picture

Did you know that Max likes fireflies? He enjoys watching them blink their bright, yellow lights off and on. Do you? Here's a fun way for you to make fireflies magically appear in your picture.

What you'll need...

- One 7x11-inch piece of white poster board or sturdy white drawing paper
- Crayons
- Paper towel
- Newspaper or brown kraft paper
- Paintbrush
- Liquid soap
- Black tempera paint
- Pencil or toothpick

1 Use a yellow crayon to draw a line across the poster board, about 3 inches from the top. Color from the top of the paper to this line with the yellow crayon. Press the crayon firmly and color very heavily so the area is completely covered.

Below the yellow area, draw a picture of your backyard, favorite playground, or park.

2 After you finish coloring, brush off any crayon flecks with a paper towel.

Cover the counter with newspaper. Mix a very small amount of liquid soap with the black paint. (The soap helps the paint stick to the waxy crayoned surface.) Use a paintbrush to paint over only the yellow part of your picture.

3 Let the paint dry thoroughly. Now fill the night sky with little yellow fireflies by using a pencil to scratch through the black paint.

If you like, you also can scratch off the shape of a moon and some stars.

Little hands can help prepare their own nutritious snack.

Night Owl Snack

Do you know what night creature makes this wonderful sound, "Whooo Hoo"? Can you guess what sound you'll make after eating this delicious snack? We think it will be, "Yum, Yum!"

What you'll need...

- Table knife
- Peanut butter or soft-style cream cheese
- Saltine or graham crackers
- Rich round or wheat crackers
- Banana slices
- Raisins or cereal

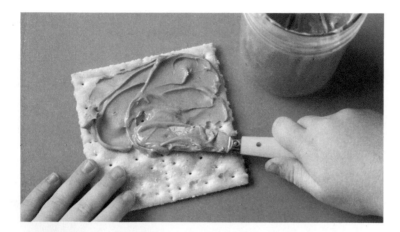

1 For the owl's head, use a knife to spread the peanut butter onto the saltine cracker.

2 To make the owl's eyes, place 2 smaller crackers and 2 banana slices on top of the cracker.
   Add 2 spoonfuls of cream cheese and top with 2 raisins (see photo).

3 For the owl's beak, use half of a banana slice. For the owl's eyebrows use cereal, if desired.
   What other creatures can you create using crackers, peanut butter, bananas, and raisins?

26

Two egg carton cups taped together become a nifty-looking bat.

Bouncy Bats

Watch out! These springy bats are coming to visit you at your home. Just how many of them show up depends on how many you make. Do you want your bat to look funny, silly, or scary?

What you'll need...

- Black construction paper
- Pencil
- Scissors

- 2 plastic foam egg carton cups
- 1 large rubber band, cut in half

- Tape
- White crafts glue
- Buttons, cereal, or shaky eyes

1 Fold the construction paper in half. Draw a bat wing on the paper. Use scissors to cut out 2 wings.

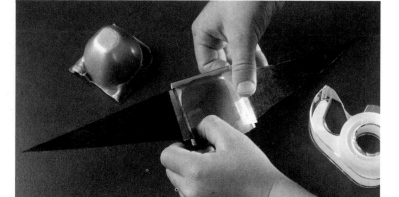

2 Put a piece of tape onto 1 end of each bat wing. Lay taped ends inside an egg cup and tape in place (see photo).

Put a piece of tape on 1 end of the rubber band. Place taped end inside egg cup between the wings. Press the tape to hold rubber band in place.

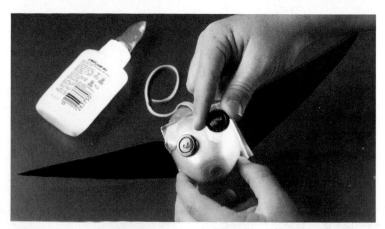

3 To make the bat's body, hold the 2 cups back to back and tape them together.

For the eyes, glue buttons onto the egg cup.

Bat Dress-Ups

Make your bat special by decorating it. Give your bat ears by cutting out small paper triangles and taping them onto the head.

Or, make a funny mouth by gluing paper, cereal, or buttons onto the face.

Make your bat pretty by coloring the wings or gluing on glitter.

Parents' Pages

We've filled this special section with more activities, recipes, reading suggestions, hints we learned from our kid-testers, and many other helpful tips.

Wake Up, Max!

See pages 4 and 5

Did your children find 11 items out of place in the picture? Here's the list of items: pepper shaker, frog in sink, strawberry drawer handle, telephone receiver, window curtains, wall clock numbers, fish on clock, flowers on stove top, window in refrigerator, toy car in dog bowl, and tennis racket for table leg.

● Reading suggestions:
Dawn by Uri Shulevitz
Aaron Awoke
   by Marilee Robin Burton

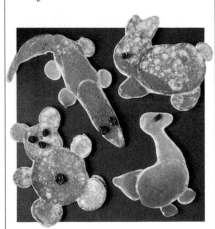

Sunshine Breakfast Biscuits

See pages 6 and 7

This tasty recipe for morning biscuits will encourage your children to eat breakfast. Here's another way to make breakfast more appealing— serve Creature Cakes.

Simply prepare your favorite pancake batter and let your children help you pour it into the special shapes on a hot griddle. A rabbit, duck, alligator, and bear are a few easy ideas to start with. Perhaps your children can think of other animals they would like to eat. Then let them add raisins, dates, or other dried fruit for the eyes, noses, mouths, and belly buttons.

Smiling Sun

See pages 8 and 9

Do your children know that the sun is a star? It is called a daytime star.

Ask your children what they like to do during the day and during the night. What can they do *only* during the day or *only* at night?

● Reading suggestion:
When the Sun Rose
   by Barbara Helen Berger

Shadows

See pages 10 and 11

A good sunny day activity for you and your children is a shadow stroll. Let your children find their shadows on the sidewalk. Compare their shadows to the shadow of a bush, street sign, or tree.

Ask them which shadow is the biggest. What happens to their shadows as they move?

Take the same walk at another time of the day and notice how the shadows have changed. Ask your children when shadows look the longest and when they look the shortest. Explain that as the sun moves during the day, shadows move, too.

Shadow Pictures

See pages 12 and 13

Here's how your children can make shadow pictures with their heads. Have each child stand near a wall so the child's shadow falls on the wall. Tape a piece of paper to the wall where the shadow of the child's head falls. Trace the shadow on the piece of paper. The finished picture makes a great gift for grandparents.

Shadow Puppets

See pages 14 and 15

Children love puppet shows, especially when shadows are the star performers. Setting up a puppet stage is simple. Have your children crouch behind a table, sofa, or other piece of furniture. Just make sure they are close to a wall so the audience can see the shadows.

● Reading suggestions:
I Have a Friend
   by Keiko Narahashi
Bear Shadow
   by Frank Asch

Sleep Tight, Max

See pages 16 and 17

Here's a kid's treat for a good night's sleep.

Good-Night Cocoa

2½ cups nonfat dry milk powder
1½ cups tiny marshmallows
1 cup sifted powdered sugar
½ cup powdered nondairy creamer
½ cup unsweetened cocoa powder
Boiling water

● In a storage container stir together milk powder, marshmallows, powdered sugar, dry creamer, and cocoa powder.
● Store the cocoa mixture, tightly covered, at room temperature for up to 3 months.
● For each serving, in a mug add ⅓ cup cocoa mixture with ¾ cup boiling water. Stir well.

Little-House Night-Light

See pages 18 and 19

Before starting this project, you'll need to do this ahead:
● Collect 1-quart milk or juice cartons. A 9x11-inch sheet of

construction paper will fit around a 1-quart milk or juice carton perfectly.
● Wash out the carton thoroughly. Use a crafts knife to cut a hole in the bottom of the carton so a flashlight will fit. Let dry.
● One side of the carton has been opened for pouring. You'll need to open up the other side. Now you and your children are ready to begin.

Instead of making a nightlight, let your children make a whole village from empty milk cartons (see photo above). Or maybe they would like to make a row of buildings that look like the ones on your street.
● Reading suggestions:
Bedtime for Frances
by Russell Hoban
Goodnight, Moon
by Margaret Wise Brown

Moon Faces

See pages 20 and 21

This homemade clay is versatile enough to use all year round. It makes party favors, Christmas tree decorations, Easter eggs, jack-o'-lanterns, flags, and birthday balloons.

When your children's baked shapes are cool, let them decorate their art masterpieces with tempera paint.

Salt Dough
1 cup water
½ teaspoon yellow food coloring or any desired color (optional)
3 cups all-purpose flour
1 cup salt

● In a 1-cup measure combine water and food coloring, if desired. In a large mixing bowl stir together flour and salt. Add water mixture. Stir till flour is moistened.
● Turn dough out onto lightly floured surface. Knead 10 minutes or till smooth.
● Place dough in a clear plastic bag. Store in refrigerator until ready to use dough.
● Before using the dough, check its consistency. If the dough is too sticky, knead in a small amount of flour. If dough is too stiff, knead in several drops of water.

Dough Tips

● For easy cleanup, be sure you have some damp washcloths or paper towels on hand for sticky little fingers.
● While your children are working with the Salt Dough, keep any unused dough covered with a damp cloth or paper towel.

Night Creatures

See pages 22 and 23

Before bedtime, sit outside with your children at different times of the year. Ask them to be very quiet and listen to the sounds around them.

Can they hear any night creatures? Which creatures can they hear? Where are the sounds coming from?
- Reading suggestions:

In the Middle of the Night
    by Aileen Fisher
Night in the Country
    by Cynthia Rylant

Firefly Scratch-Off Picture

See pages 24 and 25

Fireflies are fascinating to children of all ages. Here's a poem about fireflies to read aloud to your children:

Five little fireflies
    Went flitting one night,
    Over the hill
    And out of sight.

The first little firefly
    Sat on a tree.
The second little firefly
    Perched on a knee.

The third little firefly
    Landed on a flower
The fourth little firefly
    Climbed a tall tower.

Then Mama Firefly went
    Blink, blink, blink.
And all five flitted home
    Quick as a wink.

Night Owl Snack

See pages 26 and 27

Pinecone owls come out any time of the day. These friendly fellows are easy for your children to make, too. They only need 3 things—cotton balls, a pinecone, and pipe cleaners. Here's how:
- Slightly unravel the cotton balls.
- Gently brush the piece of cotton over the pinecone so it sticks to the cone. This should give the pinecone a soft, feathery appearance.

- Bend the pipe cleaners to form the owl's two eyes and two ears. Attach the pipe cleaners by inserting the pinecone through the pipe cleaner eyes and ears (see photo).
- Have your children name their new feathered friends. Ask them what owls like to do.

Bouncy Bats

See pages 28 and 29

These bat buddies were a big hit with our kid-testers. Some of the children even took left-over materials home with them so they could make a whole family of bats.

Be sure to save these bats and get them out again at Halloween. Let your children take them along on beggar's night. Or hang them in a window with your other Halloween decorations.
- Reading suggestions:

Billions of Bats
    by Miriam Schlein
Bats
    by Alice Hopf

BETTER HOMES AND GARDENS® BOOKS
Editor: Gerald M. Knox
Art Director: Ernest Shelton
Managing Editor: David A. Kirchner
Department Head, Food and Family Life: Sharyl Heiken

DAY AND NIGHT
Editor: Sandra Granseth
Editorial Project Manager: Liz Anderson
Graphic Designers: Harijs Priekulis and Linda Ford Vermie
Contributing Illustrator: Buck Jones
Contributing Photographer: Scott Little
Project Consultant: Lisa Ann Bielser

Have BETTER HOMES AND GARDENS®
magazine delivered to your door.
For information, write to:
ROBERT AUSTIN
P.O. BOX 4536
DES MOINES, IA. 50336

Night Creatures

See pages 22 and 23

Before bedtime, sit outside with your children at different times of the year. Ask them to be very quiet and listen to the sounds around them.

Can they hear any night creatures? Which creatures can they hear? Where are the sounds coming from?

● Reading suggestions:
In the Middle of the Night
   by Aileen Fisher
Night in the Country
   by Cynthia Rylant

Firefly Scratch-Off Picture

See pages 24 and 25

Fireflies are fascinating to children of all ages. Here's a poem about fireflies to read aloud to your children:

Five little fireflies
   Went flitting one night,
   Over the hill
   And out of sight.

The first little firefly
   Sat on a tree.
The second little firefly
   Perched on a knee.

The third little firefly
   Landed on a flower
The fourth little firefly
   Climbed a tall tower.

Then Mama Firefly went
   Blink, blink, blink.
And all five flitted home
   Quick as a wink.

Night Owl Snack

See pages 26 and 27

Pinecone owls come out any time of the day. These friendly fellows are easy for your children to make, too. They only need 3 things—cotton balls, a pinecone, and pipe cleaners. Here's how:

● Slightly unravel the cotton balls.
● Gently brush the piece of cotton over the pinecone so it sticks to the cone. This should give the pinecone a soft, feathery appearance.

● Bend the pipe cleaners to form the owl's two eyes and two ears. Attach the pipe cleaners by inserting the pinecone through the pipe cleaner eyes and ears (see photo).
● Have your children name their new feathered friends. Ask them what owls like to do.

Bouncy Bats

See pages 28 and 29

These bat buddies were a big hit with our kid-testers. Some of the children even took leftover materials home with them so they could make a whole family of bats.

Be sure to save these bats and get them out again at Halloween. Let your children take them along on beggar's night. Or hang them in a window with your other Halloween decorations.

● Reading suggestions:
Billions of Bats
   by Miriam Schlein
Bats
   by Alice Hopf

BETTER HOMES AND GARDENS® BOOKS
Editor: Gerald M. Knox
Art Director: Ernest Shelton
Managing Editor: David A. Kirchner
Department Head, Food and Family Life: Sharyl Heiken

DAY AND NIGHT
Editor: Sandra Granseth
Editorial Project Manager: Liz Anderson
Graphic Designers: Harijs Priekulis and Linda Ford Vermie
Contributing Illustrator: Buck Jones
Contributing Photographer: Scott Little
Project Consultant: Lisa Ann Bielser

Have BETTER HOMES AND GARDENS®
magazine delivered to your door.
For information, write to:
ROBERT AUSTIN
P.O. BOX 4536
DES MOINES, IA. 50336

Sleep Tight, Max

See pages 16 and 17

Here's a kid's treat for a good night's sleep.

Good-Night Cocoa

2½ cups nonfat dry milk powder
1½ cups tiny marshmallows
 1 cup sifted powdered sugar
 ½ cup powdered nondairy creamer
 ½ cup unsweetened cocoa powder
 Boiling water

● In a storage container stir together milk powder, marshmallows, powdered sugar, dry creamer, and cocoa powder.
● Store the cocoa mixture, tightly covered, at room temperature for up to 3 months.
● For each serving, in a mug add ⅓ cup cocoa mixture with ¾ cup boiling water. Stir well.

Little-House Night-Light

See pages 18 and 19

Before starting this project, you'll need to do this ahead:
● Collect 1-quart milk or juice cartons. A 9x11-inch sheet of

construction paper will fit around a 1-quart milk or juice carton perfectly.
● Wash out the carton thoroughly. Use a crafts knife to cut a hole in the bottom of the carton so a flashlight will fit. Let dry.
● One side of the carton has been opened for pouring. You'll need to open up the other side. Now you and your children are ready to begin.

Instead of making a nightlight, let your children make a whole village from empty milk cartons (see photo above). Or maybe they would like to make a row of buildings that look like the ones on your street.
● Reading suggestions:
Bedtime for Frances
 by Russell Hoban
Goodnight, Moon
 by Margaret Wise Brown

Moon Faces

See pages 20 and 21

This homemade clay is versatile enough to use all year round. It makes party favors, Christmas tree decorations, Easter eggs, jack-o'-lanterns, flags, and birthday balloons.

When your children's baked shapes are cool, let them decorate their art masterpieces with tempera paint.

Salt Dough
 1 cup water
 ½ teaspoon yellow food coloring or any desired color (optional)
 3 cups all-purpose flour
 1 cup salt

● In a 1-cup measure combine water and food coloring, if desired. In a large mixing bowl stir together flour and salt. Add water mixture. Stir till flour is moistened.
● Turn dough out onto lightly floured surface. Knead 10 minutes or till smooth.
● Place dough in a clear plastic bag. Store in refrigerator until ready to use dough.
● Before using the dough, check its consistency. If the dough is too sticky, knead in a small amount of flour. If dough is too stiff, knead in several drops of water.

Dough Tips

● For easy cleanup, be sure you have some damp washcloths or paper towels on hand for sticky little fingers.
● While your children are working with the Salt Dough, keep any unused dough covered with a damp cloth or paper towel.